GRE
EXHIBITIONS

Trevor May

SHIRE PUBLICATIONS

Published in Great Britain in 2010 by Shire Publications Ltd, Midland House, West Way, Botley, Oxford OX2 0PH, United Kingdom.
44-02 23rd St, Suite 219, Long Island City, NY 11101, USA

E-mail: shire@shirebooks.co.uk   www.shirebooks.co.uk

© 2010 Trevor May.

A CIP catalogue record for this book is available from the British Library.

Shire Library no. 495   •   ISBN-13: 978 0 74780 723 0

Trevor May has asserted his right under the Copyright, Designs and Patents Act, 1988, to be identified as the author of this book.

Designed by Tony Truscott Designs, Sussex, UK and typeset in Perpetua and Gill Sans.
Printed in China through Worldprint Ltd.

10 11 12 13 14   10 9 8 7 6 5 4 3 2 1

COVER IMAGE
The Dome of Discovery dominates the site of the Festival of Britain on London's South Bank in 1951.

TITLE PAGE IMAGE
The Great Exhibition Quadrille, by Louis Antoine Jullien (1812–60). People of all nations gather to celebrate international brotherhood and peace. In fact, the British press was highly chauvinistic.

CONTENTS PAGE IMAGE
The Millennium Dome, loved by some and derided by others.

ACKNOWLEDGEMENTS
Colin Baker, page 51; Les Chatfield, page 56; Karen Gillett, page 26 (middle); Ian Goulden, page 27 (bottom); Craig Hannah, page 53; Hartman Center, Duke University, page 22 (left); Bobo Ling, page 55 (bottom); London Borough of Brent Library Services, page 59; Mary Evans Picture Library, pages 23 (top), 27 (top right), and 28; Gideon Mendel / Corbis, page 55 (top); Ron Miller, page 58; Paul Mison (flickr.com / photos / blech), page 3; National Archives, page 21 (top); Mary F. Osborn, page 7 (top); Robert Pool's Glasgow Collection, page 7 (bottom); Science and Society Picture Library, page 13; Sleepychinchilla on flickr.com, page 61; Owen D. Smither, page 50 (bottom); Spellman Collection, University of Reading, title page; Thomas Cook Archives, page 24 (right); Victoria and Albert Museum, page 14; Victorian Studies Centre, Essex Library Services, pages 5, 9, 18 (top), 19 (bottom), 20, and 21 (bottom); Rachel Welfoot, page 26 (bottom); and Gavin Wilson, page 32 (bottom).

Shire Publications is supporting the Woodland Trust, the UK's leading woodland conservation charity, by funding the dedication of trees.

CONTENTS

INTRODUCTION

Opposite top:
North African
textiles to be
wondered at,
perhaps, but not to
be purchased.
Displays at the
1851 exhibition
were manned by
foreign nationals,
although they were
not yet seen as
exhibits in
themselves.

Opposite bottom:
Visitors examine
exhibits displayed
in the French
court at the Great
Exhibition, under
the watchful eye of
a French
policeman – one of
many foreign law
enforcement
officers who were
brought in to keep
order. The visitors
have come to see
objects; at later
exhibitions there
would also be
human exhibits to
marvel at.

THIS BOOK examines a series of great exhibitions in Britain between 1851 and 2000. Only one has ever been described as *the* Great Exhibition, and the validity of others to be included is open to debate. While there were similarities between them, each had its unique features, and must be considered in the context of its time.

The Great Exhibition at the Crystal Palace in London's Hyde Park set the pattern, but it was not the first exhibition to be held in London in the nineteenth century, and there is what might be considered a prehistory going back to the Middle Ages. In that period, the great fairs such as St Bartholomew's Fair in London, St Audrey's Fair in Ely (which specialised in cheap lace, jewellery and other 'tawdry' goods) and Stourbridge Fair in Cambridge served many of the same functions. Goods were displayed to attract interest and the placing of orders, and for immediate sale. The great fairs attracted merchants from abroad, keen to examine British goods for trade, as well as local purchasers who came to buy and to enjoy 'all the fun of the fair'. These elements of commerce and entertainment were central to the aims of the modern exhibitions, to which was added that of education.

A key difference lay in emphasis. The modern exhibitions were primarily intended to display rather than to sell. Indeed, sales within the Crystal Palace were to all intents and purposes forbidden. In 1851, visitors to the Great Exhibition had to limit themselves to window-shopping. Over the course of time increasing commercialisation crept in, with commercial interests sponsoring exhibits, or even whole pavilions. Direct sales to visitors increased, and there was a growing trade in souvenirs.

What was actually displayed at the exhibitions also underwent change. The early exhibitions almost exclusively displayed *objects*. While these continued to be central to the idea of an exhibition, other elements increasingly crept in, such as the display of *people*. Following a trend set at the Paris exhibition of 1889, the display of native peoples in their 'villages' achieved great popularity, and the more exotic the better. Such displays were prominent at the White City exhibitions, and continued down to the British

Above: The Millennium Show at the Dome illustrates how far the emphasis of exhibitions had moved from education to entertainment. However, the Show did serve a practical purpose. Every two hours it would draw in about 10,000 visitors from the dome, removing a third of the crowd, and helping to reduce queues in the exhibition zones.

Below: By the time of the Franco-British Exhibition in 1908, people had themselves become exhibits. This postcard shows the 'Senegalese village', which was in fact occupied by people of several tribal backgrounds and no common language.

The London Eye opened in March 2000. By June 2008, 30 million people had taken the ride of about 30 minutes. The Eye did for London what the Eiffel Tower had done for Paris, giving the common man a bird's eye view of the city.

Empire Exhibition of 1924–5. This broadening of scope was to continue to include the presentation of *ideas*. The Festival of Britain in 1951 celebrated 'Britishness', while the Millennium Dome contained zones as abstract as 'Faith' and 'Mind'.

The Dome was billed as the 'Millennium Experience', and the emphasis on sensation and the total experience, rather than the absorption of information, became a conscious aim of exhibition organisers, and something to be striven for. The Millennium Show in the Dome was a true spectacle – breathtakingly stunning but difficult to interpret. The aim of the Great Exhibition was to educate rather than to entertain, but when the Crystal Palace transferred to Sydenham in 1854 the entertainment aspect soon came to the fore. The Chicago exhibition of 1893 was the first international exposition to have a dedicated entertainment area, and this was soon taken up elsewhere. The Ferris Wheel made its first appearance there, and may well be what most visitors remembered. By the same token, in years to come more may remember the London Eye than the Millennium Dome. The London Eye, of course, was not *part* of the Millennium Dome but, as we shall see, the impact of the great exhibitions extended far beyond the buildings that housed them.

Not all of the great exhibitions held in Britain were located in London. Scotland, for example, hosted a number that were of particular significance, including the 1901 International Exhibition. This attracted over twice as many visitors as the Great Exhibition in 1851.

THE CRYSTAL PALACE

O N 1 May 1851, over half a million people crowded into Hyde Park, London, as Queen Victoria drove by carriage to the recently erected Crystal Palace. She had come to open the Great Exhibition. Inside the building, another 30,000 ticket-holders awaited her arrival. The Queen was greatly moved, yet only two weeks previously the Commissioners responsible for the Exhibition had announced that, for her security, the opening would be in private. There was an immediate furore. *The Times* fulminated, 'The Queen is not Lady Godiva.' The decision was revoked, but a massive security operation was mounted. The number of troops stationed in London was doubled, and a thousand men were added to the Metropolitan Police. It has to be remembered that, less than a year earlier, the Queen had been attacked in Piccadilly. Her assailant, Robert Pate, was no ruffian but a half-pay officer in the army, and the son of the High Sheriff of Cambridgeshire. Pate was deranged, but there were real revolutionaries in London, many of them refugees from the political upheavals that had swept Europe in 1848. Times were unsettled, and the decision of the Pope in September 1850 to restore the hierarchy of Roman Catholic bishops in England added to the economic and political pressures on the Government. The repeal of the Corn Laws in 1846 saw the beginning of the end of protection and the coming of free trade, issues that remained highly contentious. The Great Exhibition, said Benjamin Disraeli, leader of the protectionist wing of the Conservative party, was 'a godsend to the Government ... diverting public attention from their blunders.'

The unsettled background to the Great Exhibition has to be borne in mind, for it is often seen simply as a celebration of industrial might – Britain was already referred to as 'the workshop of the world'. However, the intentions of the Exhibition's organisers were more complex than would at first appear. The idea to hold it was not immediately embraced by the public, and the instigators faced considerable opposition from the press as well as within Parliament. That they were successful is a tribute both to the force of

Opposite:
The iron gates manufactured by the Coalbrookdale Foundry stand open for the Queen's entry on 1 May 1851. The transept was an addition to the original design, and was originally conceived to enable the preservation of a number of elm trees on the site.

9

their vision and to their political skills and determination. The success of the project is often attributed to three men: Henry Cole, Prince Albert, and Joseph Paxton.

When Henry Cole wrote his memoirs, he prefaced them with words from the Bible: 'Whatsoever thy hand findeth to do, do it with all thy might.' It was a motto that he fully lived up to, and his hands found many things to do. A civil servant, amongst whose achievements was the cataloguing system of the Public Record Office, he also worked on the introduction of penny postage. Under the pseudonym Felix Summerley, he designed highly successful, simple domestic china. He published the first Christmas card, wrote children's books as well as political pamphlets – and did everything with all his might.

Punch lampoons the suggestion that the Queen's presence at the opening ceremony of the Crystal Palace posed a security threat.

The Royal Society of Arts still occupies premises in John Adam Street, London, designed and built for it by the Adam Brothers in 1774. It was a pioneer of industrial exhibitions in Britain.

Cole was passionate about design, and felt that deficiencies in that area constituted a weakness of British industry. Exhibitions, he felt, would provide the stimulus that would impel manufacturers to make improvements. In 1845, Cole became a member of the Society for the Encouragement of Arts, Manufactures and Commerce (which became the Royal Society of Arts in 1847). The first exhibition of prize-winning models of machines was held by the Society in 1761. This was followed by others, but by the mid-1840s the Society was in serious debt, and, as much to raise money for its activities as to encourage industry, it reinstated the exhibitions. The enthusiasm of manufacturers, however, was limited, many believing that to display their products would be to expose themselves to competitors.

In 1876, the installation of the gilded statue of Prince Albert completed the Albert Memorial. It stands on the site of the Crystal Palace in London's Hyde Park. Appropriately, Albert holds a copy of the Great Exhibition catalogue in his right hand.

A. & C. Black's *Plan of London*, 1862, shows the sites of both the Great Exhibition and of the 1862 International Exhibition, which was held on land purchased using the profits of the Crystal Palace.

Nevertheless, successful exhibitions (now national rather than metropolitan in scope) were held in 1847 and 1848, by which time manufacturers had come to see the merit in participating. Buoyed up by the success of a third exhibition in 1849, the Society gave thought to a yet larger national exhibition in 1851. Cole met Prince Albert, the RSA's President, in June 1849, mainly to discuss possible locations for the proposed exhibition, but the meeting took a different turn. The Prince put his weight behind the idea that the next exhibition must be *international* in scope. When, in January 1850, a Royal Commission was set up to plan the event, Prince Albert became Chairman, and worked with untiring enthusiasm.

Contrary to our popular conception of the Great Exhibition, the idea did not immediately sell itself to the British public, and the organisers had

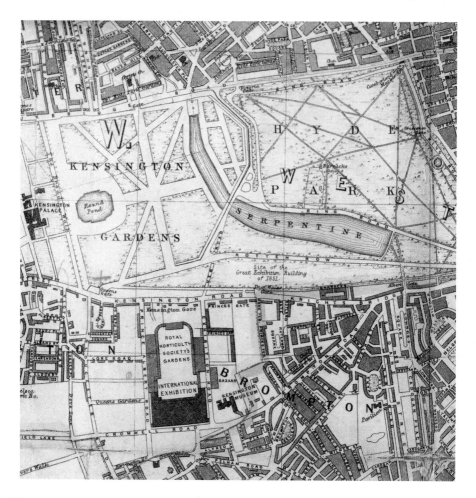

to mount a sophisticated campaign to persuade people of its merits. This meant playing up some aspects while soft-pedalling on others. For example, it was crucial to avoid any suggestion that this would be a free trade extravaganza, for that would alienate many who remained protectionist. That foreigners would be encouraged in their thousands to descend upon London filled some with horror. Foreign visitors would bring Papism, crime and disease, and would take away Britain's best ideas to copy and profit from.

One of the key questions (as it was to be with the Millennium Dome) was the choice of a site. It was assumed that London would be the venue, but where exactly? Commerce and industry had traditionally been located in the East End. To bring them to Hyde Park, in the heart of the West End, was seen as an invasion into that part of the capital city that was regarded as the province of the wealthy middle class and aristocracy. Colonel Charles de Laet Waldo Sibthorp, the MP for Lincoln, could barely contain himself (he rarely could). He advised 'persons residing near the park to keep a sharp lookout after their silver forks and spoons and servant maids'. But Hyde Park it was to be. The Exhibition Commissioners decided that they needed 800,000 square feet of exhibition space, and, on the Kensington side of the park, they were granted a two-year lease of a plot that was 2,300 feet in length and 500 feet in width.

Joseph Paxton (1801–65).
A watercolour portrait, c. 1851.

Local committees were formed in the provinces, both to select exhibits and to raise funds, it having been decided that the Exhibition was not to be a drain on the public purse. Much of the legwork needed to persuade them fully to participate fell to Dr Lyon Playfair, a chemist who had been appointed as a special commissioner to assist Prince Albert in formulating plans for the venture. He visited many industrial towns, speaking with great enthusiasm on the advantages to be gained.

With just a two-year lease on the site, the Commissioners were looking for a temporary building that could be quickly built and just as easily taken down. The Building Committee of the Royal Commission decided to run a competition for designs, and received 254, drawn from

The architectural historian John McKeen has written, 'If Paxton's sketch is a few minutes' doodle, it is one he had already spent twenty years designing.' It took only seven days to produce detailed plans, and seven weeks to come up with a full set of working drawings.

An engraving of the Crystal Palace from the Official Catalogue. The building aroused much comment, often highly critical. John Ruskin's assessment was more measured than some. He wrote, 'Largeness of dimension does not necessarily invoke nobleness of design.'

all over the world. They were satisfied with none of them, and came up with a Frankenstein monster of their own, stitching together ideas drawn from the other competitors. Disaster loomed.

Enter Joseph Paxton. The closing date for the competition had passed by the time Paxton came on to the scene. Born in 1803, the son of a Bedfordshire agricultural labourer, Paxton became the very epitome of the Victorian self-made man. Starting life as a garden boy, he rapidly rose through the ranks of his chosen trade. By the age of twenty-three he had become the Head Gardener of the Duke of Devonshire, with whom he developed a close friendship, and he came to make the Duke's Chatsworth estate the most famous garden in England. He supervised vast landscaping work, engineered the highest gravitational fountain then in existence, and experimented with the building of large greenhouses.

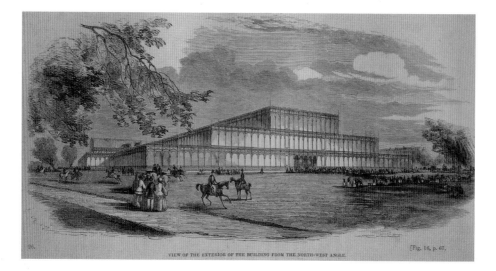

26.   VIEW OF THE EXTERIOR OF THE BUILDING FROM THE NORTH-WEST ANGLE.   [Fig. 16, p. 67.

Paxton's interests extended beyond horticulture, and he became a shrewd businessman, of whom it was said that 'he grew money as successfully as he grew flowers or trees.' Early in June 1850, he attended a disciplinary meeting of the Midland Railway, of which he was a director. Doodling throughout the meeting, he sketched – on what came to be described as the most famous piece of blotting paper in history – an idea for an exhibition building of iron and glass. Encouraged by his friends, he took just seven days to produce detailed drawings, which he sent to the Building Committee. He had great skill as a lobbyist. The plan was leaked to *The Illustrated London News*, and his friend Douglas Jerrold (a prolific contributor to *Punch*) came up with the title 'Crystal Palace'. Public support was so great that the acceptance of Paxton's plan was now assured. Two other designs incorporating iron and glass had been submitted to the Building Committee, but both had been rejected. Paxton's conception, however, was a masterpiece of prefabricated design.

The structure was designed on a modular basis, based on bays that were 24 feet wide. This resulted in a building that was 1,848 feet in length. The area covered was 19 acres, equivalent to more than six times the area of St Paul's Cathedral. To complete the job, the contractors had a mere twenty-two weeks, necessitating the most stringent critical-path planning in order to achieve a steady supply of components without the inconvenience of storage on site. From September 1850, the number of construction workers steadily built up until, by the first four months of 1851, there were on average 2,000, many of whom bivouacked in Hyde Park in the depth of winter. Chance Brothers, the Smethwick-based glass

The manufacture of the nearly 300,000 panes of glass for the Crystal Palace. This was a massive order for the time. Glass was not relieved of a crippling excise duty until 1845, and the window tax was only repealed in the year of the Great Exhibition.

Right: Much timber was used in the construction of the Crystal Palace. The roof of the transept was supported on timber trusses. Since they were wider than the transept itself, it was necessary to haul them up at an angle, with the aid of horse power.

Girders being fixed to a column, using simple blocks and tackle. Successful erection of components was dependent on highly accurate surveying for the base plates. Health and safety were a matter of personal responsibility.

manufacturers, took on foreign workers to complete the huge order for nearly 300,000 panes of glass with the unprecedented size of 49 inches by 10 inches – crucial dimensions in determining the module. The 3,300 iron columns and 2,224 girders were all tested on site prior to erection. Within eighteen hours of despatch from the foundry (also in Smethwick) the components, none of which weighed more than one ton, were being erected. Paxton once witnessed three columns and two girders going up in sixteen minutes. The most simple blocks and tackle were used, the power being provided by the combined muscles of men and horses.

The Crystal Palace was a triumph of mechanised building construction. In this engraving from the Official Catalogue, sash bars are being painted by simple machinery. When the bar was drawn out, it was 'as neatly painted as it could have been by the workman's hand'.

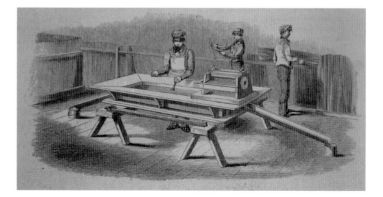

ALBERT! SPARE THOSE TREES.

ALBERT! Spare those trees,
　Mind where you fix your show;
For mercy's sake, don't, please,
　Go spoiling Rotten Row.

That Ride, that famous Ride,
　We must not have destroyed,
For, ne'er to be supplied,
　Its loss will leave a void.

Oh! certainly there might
　Be for your purpose found
A more congenial site
　Than Hyde Park's hallowed ground.

Where Fashion rides and drives
　House not industrial Art,
But 'mid the busy hives
　Right in the City's heart.

And is it thy request
　The place that I'd point out?
Then I should say the best
　Were Smithfield, without doubt.

There, by all votes approved,
　The wide world's wares display,
The Market first removed
　For ever and a day.

It is not true, as some people might think, that the Victorians paid no regard to environmental issues. The campaign to prevent the destruction of mature trees to make space for the Crystal Palace is an example of their concern for what we would now call 'green issues'. Colonel Sibthorp (*right*) was prominent amongst the conservationists.

Nevertheless, there was much mechanisation on site, especially relating to the many wooden components. Machines could cut seven or eight mortises in the time one could be cut by hand; 205 miles of sash bar were profiled by machines (designed by Paxton); and even the paint on them was applied mechanically. The Crystal Palace was a triumph of engineering ingenuity and manufacturing power, and the Official Catalogue of the Exhibition suggested that had Britain been represented by the building alone few elements in her commercial success would have been lost sight of.

The success of an exhibition is not to be measured simply by the building that houses it. What of the exhibits? There were 13,937 exhibitors, of whom 6,556 were foreign. The number of exhibits exceeded 100,000. Glance at each one for a second, and you would have spent over twenty-seven hours on

The Machinery Hall attracted many visitors, including Queen Victoria, who returned a number of times. While the machinery was impressive, a very sanitised view of heavy industry was inevitably presented.

your feet. Commentators marvelled at the comprehensiveness of the displays, but the result could be bewilderment.

The British exhibits, which occupied the western end of the Great Exhibition, were divided into four classes, broken down into thirty sections. At the eastern end, foreign countries could display their treasures as they wished, and the foreign courts proved to be particularly popular. In practice, it proved impossible to implement the classification system, as heavier exhibits were confined to the ground floor (or the exterior of the building) while lighter ones, irrespective of their class, were located on the upper galleries. Heavy machinery, whatever its function, had to be located close to the steam boilers that provided the power. All this proved confusing, and it proved difficult to move around the galleries as the catalogue might suggest. The result was a great deal of aimless (even if pleasurable) wandering. The organisers might have wished to educate the visitors, but a huge number came simply to be entertained. To use a

We might regard many of the exhibits as tacky. Yet Herr Ploucquet's display of stuffed animals shown in the Wurttemberg section required an enhanced police presence to control the eager crowds.

word that had only just gained currency, they had come as sightseers.

In April 1850, the *Economist* had argued in vain that the Exhibition should not be 'a cabinet of curiosities, or a museum of wonders, but an exhibition of what each people of the world can do to promote the ease, convenience, and happiness of themselves and others'. But people like wonders and curiosities, and these proved amongst the most popular exhibits on display. In the Wurtemburg court, extra police had to control the crowds eager to see Herr Ploucquet's display of stuffed animals playing out human lives. Count Dunin's expanding man vied with G. R. Smith's Comic Electric Telegraph, and Dr Merryweather's (leech-powered) Tempest Prognosticator, the latter so bizarre that a replica of it made its way into the 1951 Festival of Britain. And the Koh-i-Noor Diamond competed for attention with Follett Osler's 27-foot-high crystal fountain.

Industrial efficiency depends on more than brilliance of craftsmanship, dexterity and misplaced ingenuity. The new age would be governed by the market, and that market was a mass market. Many British manufacturers were angered by the decision of the Exhibition Commissioners to forbid the placing of prices alongside the exhibits, for it was in cheapness that they

Count Dunin's Mechanical Figure. The catalogue declared: 'it admits of being expanded from the size of the Apollo Belvedere to that of a colossal statue.' But how useful would it have been as a tailor's dummy, as the inventor claimed?

The Indian court proved especially popular and illustrated the opulence of the subcontinent. While the importation of Indian luxury goods, especially fabrics, had been significant in the past, India was increasingly viewed as a supplier of raw materials for British industry and as a market for its manufactured goods.

James Heath exhibited at the Crystal Palace, where he was apparently allowed to hire out Bath chairs. Like other exhibitors he was also permitted to hand out advertising material.

maintained a competitive edge. It was ironic that democratic France specialised in producing expensive goods for high society, while aristocratic Britain produced cheap goods for the masses.

In March 1851, *The Illustrated London News* published the song 'The Festival of Labour', in which one verse ran:

We strive not for dominion,
Whoe'er the worthiest be
Shall bear the palm and garland,
And crown of Victory.

Early on in their deliberations, the Commissioners had decided against offering cash prizes (the funds were not there to provide them) but instead agreed to offer medals. International juries awarded Council Medals to seventy-eight British exhibitors and fifty-four to France, which excelled in the high-quality design and manufacture of luxury goods. Prussia was awarded seven, and the United States five.

In 1847, the American poet and essayist Walt Whitman wrote:

> Yankeedoodledom is going ahead with the resistless energy of a sixty-five hundred-thousand-horse-power steam engine ... let the Old World wag on under its own cumbrous load of form and conservatism; we are of a newer, fresher race and land. And all we have to say is, to point to fifty years hence and say, let those laugh who win.

By 1897, British industrialists were, indeed, in no fit state to laugh at American (and German) competition, but in 1851, the United States was the butt of much humour. The exhibition space allotted to the Americans in the Crystal Palace was second only to that of France. They complained that they needed more – and then struggled to fill the original allotment. Nevertheless, their stand contained some of the most noteworthy exhibits of the whole exhibition. These included the McCormick mechanical reaper and the Colt revolver. The Goodyear Rubber Company mounted a display of

Top right: A lady's glove on which is printed a map of London. It does not appear to have been exhibited in the Crystal Palace, where its sale would have been prohibited, but was one of those souvenir items that was available in the capital's shops. It survives because it was submitted to the Board of Trade to gain protection under the Ornamental Design Act of 1842.

Below: The American Court, which contained some of the star exhibits at the Great Exhibition, including Hiram Powers's statue of *The Greek Slave* (right of centre).

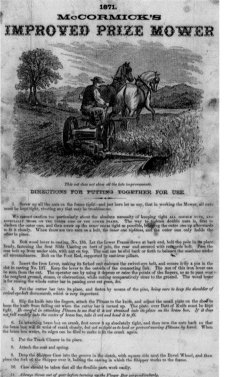

Above:
McCormick's
mechanical reaper
was one of the
most talked-about
exhibits in the
Crystal Palace. It
heralded a huge
importation of
cheap American
farming equipment
in subsequent
years.

Samuel Colt's revolvers aroused considerable interest as an example of American innovation in producing precision articles with interchangeable parts. In British industry at that time, a 'fitter' would have been required before parts could be assembled.

vulcanised rubber, and there were three exhibitors of sewing machines, patented by Elias Howe only five years previously.

The advice that *Punch* offered to the United States soon rang hollow:

By packing up the American articles a little closer, by displaying Colt's revolvers over the soap, and piling up the Cincinnati pickles on the top of the Virginian honey, we shall concentrate all the treasures of American art and manufacture into a very few square feet, and beds may be made up to accommodate several hundreds in the space claimed for, but not one quarter filled by, the products of United States industry.

On the other hand, *Punch* got it right when it came to the problem of accommodating the floods of visitors who poured into London. By the time the Exhibition closed on 11 October 1851, recorded entries to the Crystal Palace amounted to 6,063,986, a figure equivalent to one quarter of the country's population. It is impossible, however, to tell from this how many visitors were from London, or were non-resident or foreign. Figures for foreign visitors were disappointing, and in no way justified the alarm that some had whipped up beforehand. During the six months of the Exhibition,

58,000 non-Britons were recorded as having entered the country, compared with an average in the previous three years of 21,500. The vast majority of visitors were from Europe, but the failure to provide excursion trips from the Continent, and stories of the high price of accommodation in London, must have deterred many.

To help visitors to find accommodation, two registers of lodgings were created: one was set up by Matthew Digby Wyatt, an Exhibition organiser, but few landlords seem to have made use of the service, partly because it would have obliged them to fix their charges in advance. The second – a register of artisan lodgings – was organised by John Cassell, publisher of the

In July 1851 this 'New Extravaganza for the Times' transferred from the Prince's Theatre, in London, to the Edinburgh Adelphi Theatre. The entertainment was one of many examples of commercial advantage being taken of the enormous interest shown in the Crystal Palace.

THE POUND AND THE SHILLING.
"Whoever Thought of Meeting You Here?"

Above: *Punch* expresses delight at the mixing of social classes in the Crystal Palace. The 1s ticket price was set to allow artisans to attend while keeping out 'rougher' members of the working class.

Above right: Thomas Cook was a pioneer of the railway excursion. Receipts of the eight railway companies with London termini for the twenty-two weeks of the Great Exhibition were 27.6 per cent higher than in the corresponding period in 1850.

Man's Friend. A remarkable private venture of a different sort had echoes of *Punch*'s diatribe about wasted space allocated to the Americans at the Exhibition. Thomas Harrisson, owner of a large furniture depository in Ranelagh Road, Pimlico, approached the superintendent of the Exhibition with a view to storing the packing cases in which exhibits had arrived, so that they might be used again. Instead, he was persuaded to convert his premises into a temporary hostel for up to 1,000 working men and their families. Despite the fact that a remarkable range of facilities (including a daily visit to the hostel from a doctor) were available at 1s 3d per person per night, the 'Mechanics' Home', as it was called, was never more than one quarter full, and Harrisson complained about the financial ruin that he faced.

That the Commissioners were so keen to attract working-class visitors is one of the remarkable aspects of the Great Exhibition. Prince Albert had acknowledged from the outset that the involvement of the working class was crucial to success. After all, it was through the 'industry' or 'industriousness' of the workers – expressed by their skill and strength – that capitalist industry was able to develop. That most popular of Victorian popular poets, Martin Tupper, wrote of the Great Exhibition:

The triumph of the Artisan has come about at length,
And Kings and Princes flock to praise his comeliness and strength.

Prince Albert was an advocate of improved working-class housing, and was President of the Society for Improving the Condition of the Labouring Classes, which exhibited a model house, designed to accommodate four families. When the Exhibition closed, the house (designed by Henry Roberts) was re-erected in Kennington, where it can still be seen. Examples can be found elsewhere, for example in Hertford, shown here.

This was translated into twenty-five languages, including Ojibwe (although what the North American Indians made of it is not recorded). Previously, only the higher echelons had flocked to such exhibitions. Now, the workers were also invited. This was a bold social experiment, and many argued that it would lead to disaster. Paxton was howled down when he wrote to *The Times* advocating free admission for workmen, and there was a prohibition on Sunday opening – the only day when most working people might attend. What the Commissioners decided on was a sliding scale of admission prices. On the first three days that the Exhibition was open, the price of admission was kept deliberately high to enable the wealthiest to enjoy it at their leisure. On the fourth day the ticket

Below right: At the end of the Great Exhibition, the fittings and furnishings that it contained had to be disposed of. Some of the showcases, made of Spanish mahogany, found their way to the shop of Juan Floris, perfumer, in Jermyn Street, London, where they may still be seen.

The re-erected Crystal Palace at Sydenham was larger and more complex than its predecessor. It had 50 per cent more floor space, and consumed twice as much glass. There were new transepts and wings at the north and south ends. The overall aesthetic was altered by the inclusion of two huge water towers.

price fell to 5s, where it remained until 26 May, when it fell to 1s from Monday to Thursday, 2s 6d on Fridays, and 5s on Saturdays. The ticket price of 1s, which was based on no precise social analysis, was thought to be that which would allow the respectable artisan in, while keeping the riff-raff out. There was some trepidation as the first 1s day approached, and as a safeguard thirty-eight sergeants and four hundred constables of the Metropolitan Police were on duty. The day passed without incident, and the *Economist* later wrote that the British people had proved themselves to be 'a multitude without becoming a mob'. It is clear that the 4 million 1s ticket holders greatly contributed to the overall financial success of the Exhibition.

The bust of Paxton in the Crystal Palace grounds at Sydenham is one of the few reminders of the exhibition building that once stood there.

The Great Exhibition made a profit of £186,437. For his contribution, Joseph Paxton received £5,000 and a knighthood. The Commissioners had to decide what to do with the rest of the money. A number of suggestions were made, including the establishment of a national college of arts and manufactures, based on one in Paris. Eventually, with a grant from the Government to supplement the

The word 'dinosaur' had been current for little over a decade when giant reproductions of such creatures were displayed in the grounds of the Crystal Palace at Sydenham, soon after their opening. Nearly thirty of them, made of brick, iron and plaster, are still to be seen.

Above: A prize card from the National Show of Cage Birds in 1933. Such shows were regular events at the Crystal Palace, and proved very popular.

Right: A passenger aircraft on the Paris to London route flies over the Crystal Palace in this illustration from 1920. A long-standing (but groundless) conspiracy theory claimed that the disastrous fire of 1936 was deliberately caused in order to remove a prominent landmark that, in any future war, might guide enemy bombers towards London.

Exhibition surplus, two estates were purchased in South Kensington, just to the south of the Crystal Palace site. On this land were built the Science and Natural History Museums, premises for the Royal Geographical Society, the Imperial College of Science and Technology (now part of the University of London), the Royal Albert Hall, and the Victoria and Albert Museum. The laying of the foundation stone of the last named museum in 1899 was Queen Victoria's last public act. The acquisition of the valuable South Kensington estate resulted in the Royal Commission being made permanent. It still exists (and has a website) and awards research and industrial fellowships and industrial design studentships, as well as engaging in other educational work.

The Crystal Palace, however, is no more, though it did not die until 1936. All efforts to keep it in Hyde Park came to nought, and the building was purchased by a company floated by the London, Brighton & South Coast Railway, with Paxton playing a vital role. The building was dismantled and moved to Sydenham in south London, where it reopened in 1854.

If the Crystal Palace in Hyde Park had been intended to educate all classes, the Crystal Palace at Sydenham soon came to be an unashamed place of entertainment for workers and members of the lower middle class. Here they could enjoy gardens and fountains, concerts and shows, as well as exhibitions. And by 1861 they could enjoy the grounds on a Sunday, too!

A commemorative medal for the 1862 International Exhibition, the last of its kind to be held in England. The death of Prince Albert in 1861 led to the postponement of the exhibition, and cast something of a shadow over it. Nevertheless, it managed to attract more visitors than its predecessor.

Franco-British Exhibition London (Shepherd's Bush) 1908 Official Guide

PRINTED AND PUBLISHED BY BEMROSE & SONS LTD. LONDON.

1/-

THE WHITE CITY
EXHIBITIONS

B Y THE EARLY twentieth century, the Crystal Palace was becoming shabby, and the enterprise was running into financial difficulties. A brief reprieve was offered in 1911, when it hosted the Festival of Empire, held to celebrate the coronation of King George V. Three-quarter scale replicas of the parliament buildings of the dominions and colonies were constructed, together with a reconstruction of a South African diamond mine and an Indian tea plantation.

The Great Exhibition of 1851 had been organised by a Royal Commission in a highly centralised manner. The great London exhibitions of the beginning of the twentieth century were the brainchild of an entertainment impresario – the little-known Imre Kiralfy (formerly Königsbaum) who was born in Pest, Austria-Hungary, in 1845 and took British nationality in 1901. A talented dancer with a taste for music and art, the young Kiralfy started out as a child stage performer. The family moved to Berlin, and then to Paris, where in 1867 Kiralfy visited the Universal Exhibition. Later, they moved to the United States. Here (until they fell out and became rivals) Imre and his brother, Bolossy, became producers of spectacular entertainments, with lavish sets and costumes, and large casts. In 1891 he came to England, where he created Venice in London at Olympia. This event combined entertainment and education by bringing together a spectacle with an exhibition. At the Chicago World's Columbian Exposition in 1893, he put on a hugely successful show, 'America', conceived in twelve acts. Back in London in 1895 he revitalised the Earl's Court showground (opened in 1887) with the Empire of India Exhibition. Other high-profile exhibitions followed there, and he decided to give himself a larger canvas to work on by acquiring 140 acres of agricultural land at Shepherd's Bush in west London, where he laid out the White City, home to the Franco-British Exhibition of 1908. The year 1862 had seen the last truly international exhibition in England (though not in Scotland), and thereafter exhibitions were national (as in the Festival of Britain in 1951), bi-national (as in the Franco-British

Opposite:
Britannia and
Marianne together
grace the cover of
the Official Guide
to the Franco-
British Exhibition
of 1908.

Exhibition, and the Japan-British Exhibition of 1910), or celebratory of some other grouping of nations, such as the British Empire Exhibition of 1924–5.

The context of the Franco-British Exhibition of 1908 was the signing of the Entente Cordiale between Britain and France in 1904, one of a series of treaties between the Great Powers entered into before the First World War. A cartoon that appeared at the time of the Exhibition showed two puzzled Londoners gazing at a lamp-post decoration consisting of the French tricolour flag and the letters 'RF' (République Française). 'What does that stand for?' asks one. 'Real Friends,' replied the other. It was a

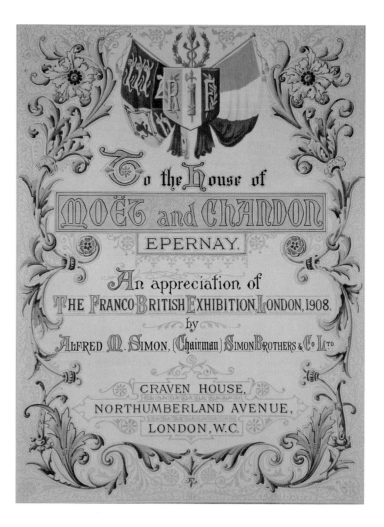

Unlike the Great Exhibition, the Franco-British and later exhibitions included commercially sponsored pavilions and stands. This illuminated dedication comes from a commemorative book produced by an English wine merchant to celebrate the great French champagne maker, Moët and Chandon, who had a pavilion at the Exhibition.

Swan Boats, Court of Honour, Franco-British Exhibition, London, 1908

The Court of Honour at the Franco-British Exhibition. As well as having a popular appeal, lakes helped drain off rainwater from exhibition grounds, and provided reservoirs in the event of fire.

good guess, for the Exhibition aimed to promote a real friendship between two nations who had historically experienced much friction. To the political *entente* was now added an economic one – an *entente commerciale* – without which the former could not long survive. It was the French Chamber of Commerce in London which came up with the proposal. Committees of the great and the good developed the idea, but Kiralfy remained the driving force in his role as 'Commissioner General'.

The Franco-British Exhibition was the largest exhibition held in Britain up to that date, and attracted well over 8 million visitors. The whole of the 140-acre site was used, of which 40 acres were covered with 120 exhibition buildings and pavilions. There were some new features, including a Palace of Women's Work, and galleries devoted to British and French fine and decorative arts. Paintings had been excluded from the Great Exhibition, unless displayed in order to demonstrate some new feature of the paint itself, but here they were given great prominence.

The exhibition buildings could hardly have been more different from the clean lines and transparency of the Crystal Palace – a

PREPARING MOULDINGS.

Craftsmen work with fibrous plaster (otherwise known as 'staff') to prepare the decorative facades of exhibition buildings. It proved a very durable building material.

The Flip-Flap was one of the crowd-pullers at the Franco-British Exhibition.

The Tunis and Algeria pavilion, one of several French colonial pavilions at the 'Franco'.

transparency that revealed the underlying framework. The whiteness of the White City was a confection of icing, covering the steel structure beneath. Flamboyant façades of fibrous plaster were designed to give a feeling of opulence and splendour. The Crystal Palace had been seen by many as a triumph of engineering rather than of architecture, whereas the engineering of the Chicago Exposition of 1893 (the original 'white city'), the Grand Palais at the Paris Exposition of 1900, and the buildings of the Franco-British Exhibition, was lost behind layers of plaster and stone. By the late nineteenth century, 'architecture', however meretricious, had triumphed. The engineering wonders were now in the amusement section of the exhibition – the Ferris Wheel, the Eiffel Tower, and the Flip-Flap respectively.

The British and French Empires were the largest in the world, and the Franco-British Exhibition proved an ideal showcase to present imperial power. Pavilions, usually built in a vernacular style, displayed (and often sold) examples of local craftsmanship. They also illustrated the range of raw materials that were vital to the economies of the colonising country. There was a strong exploitative element here, justified by contemporary views on a hierarchy of races. Paul Lafage wrote after the

'Franco' (as it soon came to be known): 'We have taught the natives to utilise those improved methods of work that our civilisation puts into their hands.' And visitors could see the 'natives' for themselves, for they could visit a 'Senegalese village'. It consisted of a number of families living in their huts, but they were drawn from several distinct regions, with no common language and with quite distinct cultures. But they were very exotic and 'ethnic', and that is what the crowds wanted. On the British side there was an Irish village – Ballymaclinton – sponsored by the Maclinton Soap Company of County Tyrone. Supposedly based on the village of Donaghmore in County Meath, Ballymaclinton was populated by 150 'colleens'. They demonstrated their simple way of life and presented a cosy image of an Ireland that, in reality, was involved in a

Above left:
The large, open-air exhibitions often provided novel forms of transport to convey visitors around the site. At the Franco-British Exhibition these included rickshaws, 'pulled by a brown clothed native at a loping trot'.

Above right: The folksiness of the Irish 'village' of Ballymaclinton at the Franco-British Exhibition to convey the image of a Britain in which the English were the dominant partners.

Kiralfy's plans for the White City included a stadium that could seat 68,000 or accommodate 130,000 standing spectators. It was closed in 1983 and demolished two years later.

Stadium, Franco-British Exhibition, London, 1908

The distance of the modern marathon was established at the 1908 Olympic Games. The race commenced at Windsor Castle and finished in front of the Royal Stand at the White City Stadium, a distance of 26 miles and 385 yards. First into the stadium was Dorando Pietri of Italy. Within yards of the finishing line, and having collapsed several times, he was assisted by two officials. As a result, he was disqualified, although he remained the hero of the day.

violent struggle over independence. Ballymaclinton was 'spick and span at every turn and twist, wide and white and clean' – and just about as real as Disneyland.

A contemporary commentator wrote of Ballymaclinton, 'the sixpence charged for admission brought it to the level of a side show.' Side shows and amusements were now central to the success of an exhibition, and the White City could boast the Flip-Flap. Sixpence spent on this would give you three minutes in a carriage accommodating forty-eight

The Flip Flap,
Imperial International Exhibition,
London, 1909

Left: The Imperial International Exhibition, held at the White City in 1909, showcased the empires of Britain, France and Russia. Many features of the Franco-British Exhibition were retained, including the ever-popular Flip-Flap.

Below: A commemorative teacup and saucer. Such items became typical of the souvenirs that were manufactured in conjunction with major exhibitions.

passengers on the end of 150-foot swinging arms that would raise you to an overall height of 200 feet. From that height (on a clear day) you could see Windsor Castle, the Crystal Palace at Sydenham, or even Wembley – where the next great exhibition would be.

In Uji Village, Japan-British Exhibition

The Japan-British Exhibition of 1910 tended to be referred to as the 'Japanese Exhibition' by British commentators as the participation of the host nation was minimal. It proved extremely popular, although the imposition in that year of new import tariffs by the Japanese government was unwelcome to British machinery manufacturers, who felt particularly discriminated against.

OFFICIAL  DAILY
PROGRAMME

3ᴰ

BRITISH EMPIRE
EXHIBITION
1924

FRIDAY

THE BRITISH EMPIRE EXHIBITION, 1924 AND 1925

O NE OF THE vice-presidents of the Franco-British Exhibition, and a member of its executive committee, was Lord Strathcona, a politician and businessman in Canada. In 1913, he donated £10,000 towards the funds to acquire the Crystal Palace for the nation, and not long before his death in January 1914 he put forward the idea of an exhibition that would be confined to the British Empire. The idea was taken up, and, but for the outbreak of the First World War, the exhibition would probably have been held at the White City, where Kiralfy's buildings were still available. During the war, the White City complex became a recruit depot, a medical inspection centre and an aircraft factory and, when the idea of an Empire exhibition was taken up again in 1919, a new site was sought.

By 1921 a greenfield site had been secured at Wembley, incorporating Wembley Park, which had been developed as pleasure grounds by Sir Edward Watkin, Chairman of the Metropolitan Railway Company. The 216-acre site was ideal for an exhibition, for the Metropolitan Railway could convey passengers from Baker Street Station in central London in only twelve minutes. Later, *The Times* was to claim that 90,000 people an hour could be delivered to the Exhibition by the various means of transport available. Construction at the site commenced in January 1922, the intention being that the grounds should contain a mixture of permanent and temporary structures. All the permanent buildings, which included Palaces of Art, Engineering, Industry, and the Government Building were to be made of ferro-concrete. 50 acres of the site were allocated to the Amusement Park, which boasted a roller coaster a mile long.

The British Empire Exhibition was opened by King George V and Queen Mary on 23 April (St George's Day) 1924. At the end of the opening speech, a message from the King was handed in at the Stadium Post Office. Transmitted by telegraph at 11.49.35, it circled the globe, to be received back at 11.50.55, 80 seconds later. In that time, it had travelled through night and day. This was the Empire 'on which the sun never sets', and to reinforce the point, in the Government pavilion there was a working illustration of the sun's vain attempt to do so.

Opposite:
The *Official Daily Programme* was an essential guide to each day's varied activities. It listed the times that bands played at nine venues in the grounds (this day's music provided by the Edmonton Newsboys' Band from Canada, and the British Guiana Military Band); various demonstrations and performances; conferences; and the evening spectacular, which on this day was 'Eastward Ho!' telling the story of South Africa and India.

Left: His Majesty's Government Building. The Official Guide observed, 'The plain portico is supported by columns 32 feet high, and the six lions guarding the entrance reduce those around Nelson's Column to mere kittens.'

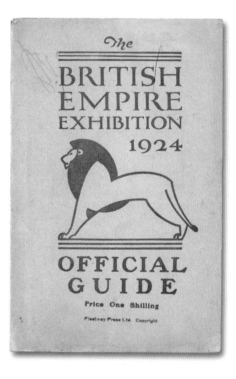

Below: The *Metro-Land* guides were published between 1915 and 1932 by the Metropolitan Railway Company to encourage housing development along their line through Middlesex, Hertfordshire and Buckinghamshire. The railway had a station next to the grounds of the British Empire Exhibition, and the Stadium featured on the cover of the 1924 edition of the guide.

The guide to the Exhibition carried the official logo – the Wembley Lion.

Crowds walk past the Australia building towards the Stadium. Many of the ancient trees in Wembley Park were retained *in situ*, while other mature trees were successfully lifted and replanted.

Over seventy dominion and colonial governments participated in the Exhibition, and their pavilions and displays were spread around the 15 miles of road across the site. From the late nineteenth century, most great exhibitions had prided themselves on novel forms of transportation for visitors, and this one was no different. Amongst the most popular was the Never Stop Railway, which could carry up to 20,000 passengers an hour. The cars engaged with a screw thread beneath the rails, and by varying the

The Admiralty Theatre in the Government Building contained a 72-foot-wide water-stage on which incidents from naval history were recreated, including the attack on Zeebrugge in the First World War.

If sculpture in butter was what you had come to see, there was a choice, with the Prince of Wales in the Canadian pavilion, and Jack Hobbs in the Australian. The craze for impermanent sculpture goes back at least to 1889, when the Americans exhibited a chocolate Venus de Milo in Paris.

pitch of the screw they could be slowed to a speed of 1½ miles an hour in stations (slow enough for passengers to board and alight) or accelerated to speeds of up to 24 miles an hour between stations. In addition, there was a rubber-tyred Road-Rail, and a fleet of two hundred Railodok electric buses.

The British Empire Exhibition brought the Empire to suburbia, but also gave the suburbanites a vision of a different way of life at home. The 1920s were a decade of great contrasts, with industrial depression and unemployment in the north, but relative prosperity in the south. The interwar years would be hard for the miners who guided visitors through the reconstruction of a coal mine in the Exhibition grounds, but they were kinder to the middle-class residents of London's new suburbs – like the ones that were growing at such speed in the Wembley area at that time. Between 1921 and 1937, 1.4 million people moved to outer London, many to work in the

The Indian pavilion was based loosely on the Taj Mahal at Agra, and the Jama Masjid mosque in Delhi. In addition, there was an Indian theatre where one could see 'snake-charmers, jugglers, and performers of a hundred mysteries that enchant the East'.

great Art Deco factories of companies such as Hoover, the vacuum cleaner manufacturers, with shining premises on the Great West Road. Those with a job might remember these years as the ones when they bought their first car, or acquired their first house. For such people there was much to excite them at the Exhibition.

In the Palace of Engineering there were motor cars galore to

For a subscription of two guineas, it was possible to receive Fellowship of the Exhibition. This entitled the holder to admission at all times, and contributed to a fund from which Empire Scholarships to the value of £1,000 were awarded to overseas students for university or technical education.

By the time of the British Empire Exhibition, the production and sale of souvenirs had become well established. Cheap transferware was always popular.

be admired. If you did not like the Austin Seven, priced at £165, there was always the Morris or the Standard. Not keen on those either? Then try the Alvis, the Beardmore, the Calcot and the Calthorpe, the Hillman, the Humber, the Lagonda, the Swift, or the Trojan. All were there, as were those of other manufacturers. And for Madam? Now that domestic servants were so hard to find in the postwar years, the lady of the house would need to do her own housework. In 1922, the first United Kingdom edition of *Good Housekeeping* appeared, with many articles on the joys of housework. Here again, the Palace of Engineering could help. As the guidebook observed, 'The electrical appliances for the home... [will] rouse envy and desire in the breast of the housewife who sees the cleanliness and efficiency of electric stoves, grills, washers, cleaners, cake-mixers, toasters, and hot bottles.'

Over 17 million visitors attended during that season, and nearly 10 million came when the exhibition reopened in 1925. It was not a financial success, however, and at the end of the day there was a deficit of nearly £2 million.

THE FESTIVAL OF BRITAIN, 1951

L IKE THE British Empire Exhibition before it, the Festival of Britain was held six years after the end of a world war, but the situations were in many respects dissimilar. The Cold War had commenced almost as soon as the Second World War ended, and since 1950 British troops had been fighting a bloody war in Korea. Wartime shortages continued and, in many respects, rationing and other economic controls became even more severe. Vast swathes of the country had been destroyed or damaged by bombing, and industries needed to be put back on their feet, especially those that could supply export markets.

Between September and November of 1946, the Council of Industrial Design mounted an exhibition at the Victoria and Albert Museum. Its title was 'Britain Can Make It' – to which wags added 'but Britain can't have it.' The 5,000 goods on display were all designed for the export market, and some 7,000 overseas trade buyers from sixty-seven countries placed orders estimated at between £25 million and £50 million.

The exceptionally severe winter of 1946–7 delayed the export drive, and the onset of recession in America in 1949 wiped out many of the earlier gains. As a consequence, the pound was devalued against the dollar, the exchange rate falling from $4.03 to $2.80. In some respects the timing of the Festival could not have been worse.

Planning had commenced a lot earlier when, in 1943, the Royal Society of Arts had raised the issue of commemorating the centenary of the Great Exhibition. In 1946 the Ramsden Committee took up the idea, and endorsed the suggestion that it should be international in scope, but this idea was dropped on grounds of cost. Under the postwar Labour Government it was to develop as a national exhibition, which in many ways could be seen as a celebration of the Welfare State. However, political sensitivities required this aspect to be under-played, just as free trade had to be played down in 1851. The Conservative Party contested the whole idea of the exhibition, and poured scorn on Herbert Morrison, the minister with special responsibility for the project. In August 1949, the *Evening Standard* hammered

Opposite:
The Festival of Britain's Skylon (shown here) seemed to float in the air. Cynics said that it was representative of the British economy in 1951 – 'it had no visible means of support'. The Skylon bore some resemblance to the Trylon at the New York World's Fair in 1939, but that had been over twice as high and had its feet planted firmly on the ground.

Above: An advertisement from *The Illustrated London News*, 12 May 1951. With strict government production controls still in place, and exports a priority, domestic customers are warned that supplies for the home market are limited.

'Mr Morrison's multi-million-pound baby'. The budget was, in fact, £12 million, although £1 million was lopped off this after the 1949 financial crisis. Still, it was argued by many opponents that, since so many houses needed to be built, and the national infrastructure required restoration and upgrading, any diversion of funds, materials or skilled manpower to the Festival was unjustified.

Plans for tented and reusable structures to be installed in Hyde Park were considered and abandoned, and a site on the South Bank of the river Thames in the heart of London was eventually selected. The chosen site was relatively cramped and was dissected by a multi-tracked railway, but it had the advantage that much of it had already been cleared of buildings by the Luftwaffe. Some further demolition was necessary, but an early-nineteenth-century shot tower was left as a link with the past. On the top was placed a lighthouse beacon (the optics made by Chance Brothers, who produced all the glass for the Crystal Palace) while on top of that a radio beacon beamed signals to the moon that were received back at a receiver in the Dome of Discovery two and a half seconds later.

In overall charge of the project was Gerald Barry, who resigned from his post as Editor of the *News Chronicle* in 1947, the year before he was appointed Director-General of the Festival. Barry had great skill as a communicator, and it was he who is credited with coining the phrase 'A Tonic to the Nation' to describe the Festival. Its aim, according to Harold Nicolson in *The Listener*, 'was to dissipate the gloom that hung like a pea-soup above the heads of the generation of 1951'. In an obituary in *The Times* in November 1968, Hugh Casson wrote of Barry that he was 'radical, deep-felt, middle-class, humorous, redolent to contemporary eyes of do-gooding and Hampstead, of petition-signing and Ealing films'. One of Barry's greatest qualities was the ability to get the best out of those who worked for him, and he brought together an impressive team.

Most of the planners were young, and many had a background in wartime propaganda or forces education, working for the Ministry of Information, the Central Office of Information and the Army Board of Education. Hugh Casson was Chief Architect, while individual sections on the South Bank were designed by, amongst others, Misha Black, Basil Spence and Ralph Tubbs. It was Tubbs who designed the Dome of Discovery, which affectionately became known to the design team as 'Ralph's Tub'. With a diameter of 365 feet, it was in its day the largest dome in the world. By way of comparison, the Millennium Dome, which in 2000 was also the largest structure of its kind in the world, was 365 *metres* in diameter.

Opposite page, bottom left: A bus ticket for one of the special routes operated during the Festival. The impact of a major exhibition on the host city's transport infrastructure is considerable, and has often created a permanent legacy.

Left: King George VI opens the Festival of Britain from the steps of St Paul's Cathedral. The choice of venue was of great significance, for wartime images of the cathedral's dome, standing proud against a backdrop of smoke and flames, seemed to sum up the fortitude of Londoners. Now they had something to celebrate.

Crowds queue to enter the Dome of Discovery. With postwar shortages, queuing was still part of everyday life for the people of Britain.

Below: This aerial view from *The Illustrated London News* shows how compact the exhibition had to be. With only 27 acres to play with (compared with 216 at the British Empire Exhibition) there was no possibility of grand vistas. However, much was made of the Thames-side site, and the river was imaginatively used to connect the South Bank exhibition with the Festival Gardens at Battersea.

Crucial to the success of the Festival was the work of James Gardner, who was a design panel member for the South Bank site, and Design Co-ordinator of the Battersea pleasure gardens. He had previously been Chief Designer of the Britain Can Make It exhibition in 1946. There he had determined to get away from the idea of objects in rows of showcases. Writing in 1983, Gardner recalled:

> ... instead of presenting goods to the eye, as in an open market – and that is how exhibitions had evolved – I tucked them round corners, behind screens and in little enclaves, so at first the visitor would see

The symbol of the Festival of Britain was designed by Abram Games (1914–96). As an official war poster designer, he produced around one hundred pieces, including the 'Blonde Bombshell', a 1941 recruiting poster for the women's Auxiliary Territorial Service (ATS), subsequently withdrawn for being too glamorous. The profile of that poster bears a strong resemblance to the 1951 logo shown here.

The aircraft carrier HMS *Campania* was loaned to the Festival of Britain for use as a floating exhibition. Flags and bunting were very much part of the overall Festival décor. Those able to read naval signal flags could have deciphered the message posted on the outside door of the toilets – 'I have sprung a leak.' While the *Campania* cruised the coast of the United Kingdom, a Land Travelling Exhibition took the Festival to the English provinces.

lots of 'décor' but no goods – wouldn't even notice if there were no goods at all. This introduced a surprise element.

Gardner's innovation, whereby the visitor was directed from one area to another, with new vistas opening out along the way, became central to the South Bank exhibition.

Barry was a newspaper man. He was a communicator who put his faith in narrative. But what was the story that the Festival set out to tell? The focus was to be on 'The Land' and 'The People'. This division made capital out of one of the site's great disadvantages – it was divided by a railway line. The designers decided to devote an upstream circuit to 'The Land' and the downstream circuit to 'The People', with pavilions located accordingly. The intention was to highlight the British people's common character, traditions and history. In his article in *The Listener*, Harold Nicolson wrote of the planners:

At the Festival of Britain, education and entertainment were kept quite separate, with the Festival Gardens and funfair located upstream at Battersea. Much that was there was intentionally whimsical, such as Roland Emett's Far Tottering and Oyster Creek Railway, based on cartoons in *Punch*.

Let us, they said … emphasize our unity. Let us show the world that we are after all a people, cemented together by the gigantic pressures of history … One thing, an indestructible thing, we all have in common, whether capitalist, bourgeois or proletariat: we have the same sort of character underneath. We are an ancient people, formed of many obscure strands. We take a pride in our … wonderful fusion of tradition and invention … of uniformity and eccentricity. Surely that also was one of the motives of the Festival to remind us that we were very, very old and very, very young. (Quoted in Conekin, page 84)

Straightforward though this view seems to be, it carried many implications for the exhibition planners. It contains many echoes of wartime propaganda praising the qualities for which the British were fighting. Humphrey Jennings was the producer of many films in this vein, and in *Family Portrait*, the last film that he completed (in 1950, just before his death), he explored the themes of the forthcoming Festival. In it he referred to the inequalities created by industrialisation, describing them as 'rifts in the family we are still having to repair'. But it was not the intention of the Festival to reopen such rifts, with the consequence that the Industrial Revolution and the Victorian 'Workshop of the World' were largely ignored. Indeed, it was almost at the eleventh

The monumental statue *The Islanders*, by the Austrian-born sculptor Siegfried Charoux, stood outside the Sea and Ships pavilion, overlooking the Thames. Britain's island history was a theme of the Festival, which was in every respect insular. In 1951, Britain was turning its back on the Empire (or Commonwealth, as it was now called), while not turning its face to Europe.

hour that it was recalled that the Festival had been intended to celebrate the centenary of the Great Exhibition, and Hugh Casson, with no budget to cover it, hurriedly put together a small pavilion. Nor, amongst all the talk of Britain being a nation of immigrants, was any attention drawn to recent immigration from the Commonwealth, despite the landmark event of the arrival of the *Empire Windrush*, bringing the first large group of immigrants from Jamaica in 1948. The emphasis, instead, was on the 'timeless past' – in other words, on the Normans and on the waves of immigration even before them.

This somewhat cosy view of 'Britishness' was most plainly portrayed in the popular Lion and Unicorn pavilion. The guidebook explained that the

The Sea and Ships pavilion, designed by Basil Spence and Partners, was highly regarded, and elements of it seemed to foreshadow Coventry Cathedral, the commission for which was awarded to Spence in 1951. The art critic William Feaver has argued that 'Coventry Cathedral marks the apotheosis of the Festival' and became 'the Mecca of the Festival Style'.

The Dome of Discovery and the Skylon seem to endorse the latest Ariel model. Back in the 1920s, two-fifths of British motorcycle production had been exported, and there were hopes in the years after the Second World War that they might be at the forefront of the export drive. Their days were numbered, however, and it was not long before Japanese machines were flooding the country.

pavilion's title 'serves to symbolise two of the main qualities of the national character: on the one hand, realism and strength, on the other, fantasy, independence and imagination'. The radio commentator Audrey Russell wrote that there was:

... an unerring touch in the choice of objects and in their juxtaposition. I can remember a 365-day clock by Thomas Tompion, an original edition of Dr Johnson's Dictionary, an edition of Shakespeare, one of the Bible, a tailor's pinking scissors, a model of the White Knight, with acknowledgments to Sir John Tenniel, and a corrected page proof of Winston Churchill's *History of the Second World War*.

Here was an attempt to communicate ideas – the English language, the British constitution, the judicial system, freedom of the press and of religion, and female suffrage. Overhead was a soaring flight of white doves, apparently released from their cage by the great straw figure of the unicorn. The pavilion was not overloaded with exhibits (indeed, the whole South Bank exhibition had only one-fifth of the number of exhibits that were crammed into the Great Exhibition), but the captions and commentary were written by the poet Laurie Lee.

Ernest Race (1913–64) was one of Britain's finest furniture designers and exhibited a chair of cast aluminium and laminated plastic at the Britain Can Make It exhibition in 1946. In 1950 he was commissioned to design the outdoor chairs for the South Bank terraces. This resulted in the Antelope chair, shown here. Made of steel, with a bent plywood seat, it became a design classic and continues in production to this day.

The Festival of Britain mobilised a great body of creative talent – architects, designers, engineers, film-makers, furniture-makers, landscape gardeners, poets and painters, sculptors, typographers – but not a single historian. What started out as a commemoration of the Great Exhibition certainly touched upon the past yet, largely as a result of Barry's insistence, set its eye resolutely upon the future. But what impact, if any, did the Festival have on the future? One area in which its influence appears to have been significant was in the field of design, where a definite 'Festival Style' is said to have emerged. William Feaver claimed that the Festival of Britain seemed to sum up what people saw as 'contemporary design':

> Braced legs, indoor plants, colour-rinse concrete, lily-of-the-valley splays of light bulbs, aluminium lattices, Cotswold-type walling with picture windows, flying staircases, blond wood, the thorn, the spike, the molecule: all became the Festival Style.

It was a style that could easily be imposed on the past. A sheet of hardboard could transform a Victorian panelled door, and a lick of bright paint could bring about a domestic metamorphosis. The style could soon become a cliché.

The Festival of Britain was fun while it lasted, and 8.5 million people were drawn to the South Bank. Just over three weeks after the Festival closed, the Labour Government was thrown out at a general election. The Conservatives came to power, and quickly set about clearing the site, ostensibly to prepare it for a Coronation Garden. The Festival Hall remained (this had been a London County Council project), and the Telecinema eventually became the National Film Theatre. But the Skylon and the Dome of Discovery are no more.

THE MILLENNIUM DOME: A GREAT EXHIBITION?

IN FEBRUARY 1998, Prime Minister Tony Blair declared that the planned Millennium Dome would be 'the envy of the world'. He went on, 'This is Britain's opportunity to greet the world with a celebration that is so bold, so beautiful, so inspiring that it embodies at once the spirit of confidence and adventure in Britain and the spirit of the future of the world.' There would of course be critics. He continued:

> It does not surprise me that the cynics have rubbished the idea. They are in good company. They are part of an inglorious strand of British history: like those who said St Paul's would be a calamity, that the 1851 exhibition would have no visitors and that the 1951 Festival of Britain would never be finished on time.

Mr Blair was fully aware that St Paul's Cathedral had *not* been a calamity; that the 1851 exhibition *did* draw in visitors (almost as many in five months as the Dome would in a year – and from a population less than half the size); and that the Festival of Britain *was* finished on time. But while his three historical examples turned out to be successes, the Millennium Dome has continued to be regarded by many as a failure. In December 2000, the *Sunday Express* suggested that, 'In 12 traumatic months [it] went from being Britain's great white hope to its great white elephant.' Even Blair had changed his mind by then: 'Hindsight is a wonderful thing, and if I had my time again I would have listened to those who said governments shouldn't try to run tourist attractions.' His choice of words is telling. A great exhibition needs to attract visitors, but it is more than just a visitor attraction, and the aims of exhibition organisers since 1851 have reflected this. Not that any of the exhibitions hitherto described had a *single* aim. They were planned to educate, to stimulate and to celebrate, as well as to entertain. They shared the lofty ideals that Mr Blair outlined in February 1998. They were more than content to attract tourists, but they were not planned primarily as tourist attractions.

Opposite:
Attaching the main cables to the towers of the Millennium Dome, early in 1998. Around one hundred climbers and abseilers were employed to install the 72 kilometres of cable net and the plastic roof.

The Dome in 2009. In October of that year, the remainder of the 999-year lease of the O$_2$ Arena, housed within, was purchased for £24 million by Trinity College, University of Cambridge, enabling the College to collect rents linked to ticket sales.

It was inevitable that the Millennium should be marked in some way, as indeed it was throughout the world. Since 1928, an international agreement, the Convention of Paris, had laid down rules for international exhibitions and world fairs, and in 1931 the Bureau International des Expositions was set up as a regulatory body. The Bureau designated Hanover as the location of what came to be seen as the Millennium Exposition. It turned out to be a disappointment. Britain had a pavilion there, in which 'a touch of eccentricity [was] thrown in for good measure', but the United States was not represented, Congress having rejected the funding. Only 18 million out of the expected 40 million visitors turned up.

The real springboard for the celebrations to mark the Millennium was the National Lottery Act of 1993, which established a lottery, the proceeds of which were to be used for a variety of purposes connected with the arts, sport and national heritage. Special provision was made for 'projects to mark the year 2000 and the beginning of the third millennium', and a Millennium Commission was set up to plan how the money should be spent. It received

The interior of the Millennium Dome. One of the dominant exhibits was the Body Zone: 'Two seven-storey-high figures – one male, one female – lean towards us as they rest on one elbow.' The Body Zone was one of the first things that visitors encountered, and proved very popular.

grants from the Lottery until April 2001, and the Commission was not abolished until November 2006, by which time over £2.3 billion of funding had been distributed.

The task facing the Commissioners was a daunting one, and when they set to work in 1994 the idea of an *exhibition* came very low down on the agenda. There was much more enthusiasm for local projects. Only Simon Jenkins, the writer (and great fan of the Festival of Britain), and the

Ron Mueck's 4.9-metre-high sculpture *Boy* featured as part of the Mind Zone. All the zones had commercial sponsors, those for Mind being BAE Systems and Marconi.

A desire to illustrate links between an exhibition and its predecessors has often been strong. The Millennium Dome contained one of the London buses, adapted as tourist offices, sent around Europe to drum up interest in the Festival of Britain. A less tangible (but more significant) link between the two events was a personal one. Peter Mandelson, Labour minister in charge of the Dome, was the grandson of Herbert Morrison, who was given responsibility for the 1951 Festival.

Conservative politician Michael Heseltine showed any real enthusiasm for an exhibition, and even they disagreed on the aims, with the former wanting a 'spectacular' while the latter favoured a trade fair.

The project soon came to possess the qualities of a Kafka novel. By law, the Millennium Commission was not able to take any financial risks itself, and had to rely on its ability to attract commercial sponsors. Its job was to support projects that were brought before it, but it could not directly initiate projects. Although it had ideas about what was needed, its task was to suggest, to persuade and to cajole. Gradually the idea of a central event took hold. 'Experience' was the buzz word at this time, with many museums around the country re-branding themselves as the 'This or That Experience'. So, the idea of the Millennium Experience was born. But where would the 'Experience' be held, and what would it be about?

One possible site that had much to recommend it was the National Exhibition Centre (NEC), on the edge of Birmingham. There were good road and rail links, and it could tap a huge population within a journey time of two hours. Furthermore, since its opening in 1976, the NEC had built up an established management with a good track record in organising big events. For all other venues an operator would have to be selected from those who might put themselves forward. The other venue that stood out was 294 acres of land on the Greenwich peninsula, which formed part of over 1,000 acres of derelict land in the borough. The site had more than the Great Exhibition's elm trees to contend with. For centuries it had been the home of noxious industries, and it was heavily polluted. To add to the problems, there were perhaps thirty unexploded Luftwaffe bombs lying beneath the surface.

For a Government enthusiastic for 'regeneration', the very dereliction of the site had a certain political attraction. Its inaccessibility would be reduced by an extension to the Jubilee Line, and there was the inevitable pull of a London location. In the event, Greenwich won the day, and in July 1997 the Commission awarded a grant of £449 million to the New Millennium Experience Company to mount and run the show.

The idea of a Dome surfaced in May 1996. The financial risks were high, and, because of the difficulty of finding sponsors, the development of the idea became what was essentially a Government project – with the added complication that the Government changed in 1997, when a Labour landslide drove out the previous Conservative administration. The new Government was initially ambivalent about the project, but eventually put its weight behind it, with Peter Mandelson (Herbert Morrison's grandson) becoming the minister in charge.

Like the Crystal Palace, the Millennium Dome was a state-of-the-art building but, unlike its predecessor, and despite its tent-like appearance,

Tributes to Michael Jackson outside the Dome in June 2009. His death occurred shortly before he was due to give a comeback performance at the O2 Arena. Just as the Crystal Palace became a centre for popular music after its transfer to Sydenham, so, too, has the Dome become a major concert venue.

Paxton's Crystal Palace left an immediate legacy in much railway architecture. When Paddington Station was rebuilt between 1850 and 1854, Brunel designed a roof of wrought iron and glass, on cast-iron pillars, with a total span of 240 feet. The legacy was short-lived, however, and the value that Victorians placed on solidity soon re-exerted itself. Not until the twentieth century was the Crystal Palace seen as a precursor of the modern movement in architecture.

was intended to be permanent rather than temporary. The Dome straddled the Greenwich Meridian, which had a certain symbolic significance. It was as if to say, 'The new millennium starts here' (though purists argued that it did not start until 2001, after the party was over). But this fact of geography gave rise to 'Time' as an appropriate theme for the event. This was later dropped, in favour of 'who we are, what we do and where we live', which were explored in fourteen zones within the Dome. The zones were to offer 'experiences' and that meant interactive technology, fit for the digital age. Unfortunately, at any one time, much of the equipment did not work! Independent surveys showed that most people professed to have enjoyed their day out at the Dome. But does that make it 'a great exhibition'?

How is the success of *any* exhibition to be judged? The first thing to ask is whether it achieved its aims. This is not always easy to answer, either because there were numerous aims, or because precise aims are hard to identify. In the case of the Great Exhibition, Henry Cole stressed the need to improve Britain's industrial design, while Prince Albert emphasised the Exhibition's capacity to make peace and brotherhood blossom.

There is not much evidence that Britain's industrial design did improve as a result of the Great Exhibition, but the economy expanded where the nation had a marked advantage – not in the production of luxury goods for a limited market, but in cheap production for a widening market. Those who were gaining a foothold in the consumer market were quite content to have cheap, machine-made copies of the goods previously available only to the wealthy. The over-decoration derided by the critics had a positive appeal to those whose austere lives had denied them access to such things. Even with cheap goods, Britain would soon face competition, and by the end of the century there was great concern at the importation of even cheaper German manufactures – a concern not shared by those who could afford to buy for the first time. The Great Exhibition was seen by some almost as a temple of consumerism, and it is an interesting thought that, in architectural terms, one of the significant spin-offs from the Crystal Palace is the shopping mall, itself evolving from the later nineteenth-century department store. William Whiteley (the 'Universal Provider') was inspired by the Great Exhibition, which also enhanced the fortunes of a little-known Knightsbridge grocer, H. C. Harrod.

Prince Albert's aims for the Great Exhibition were perhaps loftier, but was the era of peace and brotherhood that he foresaw ushered in? Even as the visitors flocked to Hyde Park, Britain was at war, engaged in the eighth of a long series of wars with the Kaffirs in South Africa (now known as the Xhosa, or Cape Frontier Wars). In December 1851, Louis Napoleon organised a coup in France, in which a number of insurgents were covered in a carpet that had been exhibited at the Crystal Palace, and shot. Two years later the Crimean War broke out, and when the Royal Small Arms Factory at Enfield was extended in 1856 the new machinery came not from Sheffield or Manchester, but from Windsor, Vermont – produced by the American firm of Robbins & Lawrence, exhibitors at the Great Exhibition.

But, for all that, it is hard to deny the Great Exhibition its unique epithet. As to other exhibitions fulfilling their aims, the Franco-British Exhibition did cement relations between the two countries that, six years later, would be fighting alongside each other in the trenches of the First World War. The British Empire Exhibition of 1924–5 kept alive interest in the Empire during the troubled economic times of the interwar period, and may have done a little to lend support for the Imperial Preference tariff scheme negotiated at Ottawa in 1932. The final imperial fling is much less well known in England, and that was the Empire Exhibition in Glasgow in 1938.

The nearest London got to the Eiffel Tower was 'Watkin's Folly' (on what later became the site of the British Empire Exhibition). Commenced in 1892, if completed it would have been 150 feet higher than its Parisian rival. But it never got beyond this first stage, and this was blown up in 1907.

Punch reflects on the Eiffel Tower, which was a permanent legacy of the 1889 Paris International Exhibition.

Basil Spence was one of the architects at that exhibition. He reappeared in 1951 at the Festival of Britain. If that was meant to be a 'Tonic to the Nation' it probably succeeded. The bad times of the war and postwar period were not over, but at least for a few months Britons could enjoy themselves – and perhaps become inspired to 'modernise' their surroundings.

And the Dome? As a 'great exhibition' the majority would probably give it the thumbs down. The building was exciting, although the writer and film-maker Iain Sinclair described it as 'a poached egg designed by a committee of vegans'. There were, perhaps, too many committees, with competing visions, for The Millennium Experience to be a great success. But we must remember all the other projects funded by the Millennium Commission. These may prove to be the real legacy.

The Millennium Commission funded 220 local projects on over 3,000 sites. One such was the Eden Project at St Austell in Cornwall. Constructed in a disused china clay quarry, the Eden Project boasts the two largest conservatories (known as biomes) in the world. Opened fully in March 2001, in its first two years Eden brought in an additional £300 million to the depressed Cornish economy. Of the total project cost of £116 million, the Millennium Commission put up £59 million.

FURTHER READING

Auerbach, Jeffrey A. *The Great Exhibition of 1851: A Nation on Display*. Yale University Press, 1999.

Briggs, Asa. *Victorian Things*. Batsford, 1988.

Colquhoun, Kate. *A Thing in Disguise: The Visionary Life of Joseph Paxton*. Fourth Estate, 2003.

Conekin, Becky. *'The Autobiography of a Nation': The 1951 Festival of Britain*. Manchester University Press, 2003.

Davis, John R. *The Great Exhibition*. Sutton Publishing, 1999.

Evans, Godfrey. *Souvenirs*. HMS Publishing, 1999.

Gibbs-Smith, C. H. *The Great Exhibition of 1851: A Commemorative Album*. HMSO, 1950.

Gloag, John (new introduction). *The Crystal Palace Exhibition Illustrated Catalogue, 1851*. Reprinted, Dover, 1970.

Green, Oliver (new introduction). *Metro-Land. British Empire Exhibition Number*. Reprinted, Southbank Publishing, 2004.

Greenhalgh, Peter. *Ephemeral Vistas: The Expositions Universelles, Great Exhibitions and World's Fairs, 1851–1939*. Manchester University Press, 1988.

Hewlett, Geoffrey (editor). *A History of Wembley*. Brent Library Service, 1979.

Hobhouse, Christopher. *1851 and the Crystal Palace*. John Murray, 1950.

Hobhouse, Hermione. *The Crystal Palace and the Great Exhibition*, Athlone Press, 2002.

Howarth, Patrick. *The Year is 1851*. Collins, 1951.

Jackman, Anna. *EXPO: International Expositions, 1851–2010*. V&A Publishing, 2008.

Knight, Donald R., and Sabey, Alan D. *The Lion Roars at Wembley*. Donald R. Knight, 1984.

Leapman, Michael. *The World for a Shilling*. Headline, 2001.

Leith, Ian. *Delamotte's Crystal Palace: A Victorian Pleasure Dome Revealed*. English Heritage, 2005.

Luckhurst, Kenneth W. *The Story of Exhibitions*. Studio, 1951.

McKeen, John. *Crystal Palace: Joseph Paxton and Charles Fox*. Phaidon, 1994.

Nicolson, Adam. *Regeneration: The Story of the Dome*. Harper Collins, 1999.

Perkins, M., and Tonkin, W. E. *Postcards of the British Empire Exhibition, Wembley*. Exhibition, 1994.

Sinclair, Iain. *Sorry Meniscus*. Profile Books, 1999.

Tongue, Michael. *3D EXPO 1862* (with stereoscope viewer). Discovery Books, 2006.

Young, Paul. *Globalization and the Great Exhibition: The Victorian New World Order*. Palgrave Macmillan, 2009.

FILM
Humphrey Jennings's film *Family Portrait*, together with three other films on the Festival of Britain and its context, is available on DVD: *London in Festival Year, 1951*. Panamint Cinema, 2009.

WEBSITES
Bureau of International Expositions: www.bie-paris.org
Construction of the Crystal Palace:
    www.vam.ac.uk/collections/periods_styles/19thcentury/crystal/
    index.html
Crystal Palace Foundation:
    www.crystalpalacefoundation.org.uk
Day at the Great Exhibition:
    www.vam.ac.uk/collections/periods_styles/19thcentury/great_ex/
    modem.html
Exhibition Study Group:
    www.studygroup.org.uk
Festival of Britain Society:
    www.whitstablepier.com/fob
Franco-British Exhibition, 1908:
    www.archive.org/details/francobritishexH00franrich
History of the Crystal Palace:
    www.news.bbc.co.uk/local/london/hi/people_and_places/history/
    newsid_8082000/8082928.stm
Millennium Commission:
    www.millennium.gov.uk/index.html
Millennium Dome: a Collection:
    www.dome2000.com/index.html
Royal Commission for the Exhibition of 1851:
    www.royalcommission1851.org.uk

INDEX